THE
POETJOURNALIST

THE
POETJOURNALIST

Aaron P. Dworkin

LENOX AVENUE
PRESS

The Poetjournalist

Published by Lenox Avenue Press

Library of Congress Control Number: 2023934228

ISBN (hardcover): 9781662938368
ISBN (paperback): 9781662938375
eISBN: 9781662938382

For Afa, Noah and Amani

There is no destination
For the leisurely words
I have to offer
Without the love
I have of you
Enveloping them
With meaning.

Table of Contents

1. SETTING THE STAGE — 1

Poetjournalist 2
Trojan Horse 4

2. ON INEQUALITY — 7

Zip Code 8
Neglect 10
For Us By Us 12
East of the River 14
A Shift Toward Justice 16
Poverty of Compassion 18
Garden of Brightmoor 19
Maternal Instincts 22
Refugee 24
Indigenous 25
Still They Fight 26

3. ON THE BLACK EXPERIENCE — 29

Mahogany Stories 30
The Green Book 34
Pulse of My People 36
A Pryor Love 40
Negro 42
The Sound of Martin Luther King 44
28 Days 46
MLK Day 48
Obama 50
First Fruit 52
The Boy King 54
Espresso 56

4. ON MY IDENTITY — 59

They Said I Wasn't Really Black 60
Nigel 63
Picture Perfect 64

Gram 68

The Road Not Taken 70

My First Teacher 72

Stealing 20s 74

Dachau 76

The Coming 78

Music of You 82

Garage Cigarette 84

Nugget 86

Baby Next Door 88

The Waiting Room 90

My Birmingham Belle 92

The Holidays 95

5. ON THE ARTS   97

Ovation 98

Rise 102

The Arts 106

String Theory 108

The Melody of Parents 110

Replay 112

Masterpiece 114

Music Teachers 116

Rosin 118

Vibration 120

Roadmap 122

Gospel Music 124

Intrigue 126

6. ENCORES   129

Whispered Journey 130

The Peace Prize 132

Winter Mind 136

ABOUT THE AUTHOR   139

SETTING THE STAGE

Poetjournalist

I am the multi-colored tubes looping down the wall
Darting around outlets colored red and yellow
Snaking into veins of the elderly woman
Gasping from within the sheets of her Covid bed
Anchored by technology to the protocols of strangers
Dedicated to prolong the life she faces
Without the grip on her lover's wrist.

I am the passive man in straight black pants
With my untucked white shirt
Facing the column of tanks as their turrets salute my defiance
In Tiananmen Square before my movement falters
Showcasing my human right to exist
My freedom to persist.

I am the failed bank filled
With the empty paper and promises of people's dreams
Chosen for their inability to pay like the stray gazelle
On the Savanna as the lion poaches their prey
In the early morning mist.

I am the twin towers twisted metal
Exploding into crimson blossoms
Fading into black entrails and futures lost
Shading the horizon of our lives like
The passions of lovers before they fall into disarray
And forget what sparked their rise and hatred of their demise
And events regretted yet still reminisced.

I am the 9 minutes and 29 seconds
That a black man donning a black tank top
Felt the knee of dispassionate authority on his full-throated neck
Before his life with voice was ground into silence that was heard
And shook the sugar maple trees of Richmond Virginia
And broke the blue wall more than any afro pick with fist.

I am the grist for bottled water office talk
I assist the memory to feel the moments lost
I am the emotion of every story missed
I am the words the newsprint failed to list
I am our soul we must enlist.

I am the Poetjournalist.

Trojan Horse

Parents of science
And the neurology of the academy
I was a sphere of spontaneity
Only found in the nature they did not study
But would... through me.

The blackness of my skin
Bled through alabaster absolute minds
With melodic cacophony on my violin
Evolving them... maturing me.

I despised as a boy
The difference, ostracized
For mulatto verse and afro art music
Alone in a land of Troy.

Adolescent disparity built
The floors on which I design
I am the artist, the Trojan Horse
Charting my course
Through corporate corridors.

A force to be reckoned
Once beckoned, emptied
They freed my soldiers of creativity
Within the walls of their city
My voice, turning corporate prose to poetry.

While intention imported my presence
Within aristocratic gates
Of marketing, finance and technology
They view me unsuspectingly
Unlike a gift from the enemy.

Opened, surprisingly
They welcome my soliloquy of sensibility
Of the human condition.

In printed sheets of quarterly accomplishments
I see sacrifice and beauty in camaraderie
Of a species who spend more time
With those who aren't family
Yet connection of accomplishment
Brings impact on community.
I gaze beyond the uniformed unanimity
Encouraging originality
Bringing safety from conformity
Realizing unity in LED lit
Paper cups and coffee machines.

I am the engineer softening
The hardware of human capital
Elocuting an efficiency that formulas
And a strategic plan never does.

Aesthetic impact institutionalized
Through alliteration with outstretched palms
My pen and meter my artistic alms
Helping humans be human again.

There is a silence in my morse code
That forbodes my role as a resource
Throat hoarse, yet body in balance
Embedded,
My artistic concourse a renaissance
Catalyzing a source of excellence.

I am The Trojan Horse.

ON INEQUALITY

Zip Code
(Commissioned as Poetjournalist-in-Residence of The Rodham Institute)

If I am endowed with rights
unavailable for abdication
For my life, liberty and pursuit of happiness
Why does geography chart a navigation
Towards my inequality?

Less than the distance
Patrick Mahomes can cast cowhide
From the seat of our democracy
27 years defines the difference
Of life expectancy from those
East of the River to the hill diners
Devouring their fare in the Capitol Grille.

20373 and 2 triple zero 7
Divided by merely 6 miles of terraced humanity
And a river equality cannot negotiate
Polluted with the sewage of hate and indifference.

3 busses keep me from my Covid doctor
And the mall where anchor stores and humanity
Serve as the remedy for my mental health disease.

Those who think I choose
To stride on broken streets with no sidewalks
Should spend a day born in a hospital ward
In 20373 then fight the homicide
Heart disease from guilty snacks at the neighborhood store
And unexpected injuries from a life lived
Without the luxury and safety of an unweighted zip code.

I am asking for the rights endowed me
For there is only so much suffering
Before subjugation is overtaken
By a passion to take
What should have been given
If we were all equal
In our most important
Independent
Declaration.

Neglect

(Commissioned as Poetjournalist-in-Residence of The Rodham Institute)

I was always last to be picked
For dodgeball in gym
After a sincere coach
Recovered me
From the deluge of twinkies and cloves
Smoked at the homeless hotel
that served as my refuge
Sophomore year
Liberating from parents focused
On a birth son
and academic publishing.

Society tells us
All politics is local
But my climate change
Wasn't global when the plant
Poured its poison
Decades before decadent
Paris hotels served up
Delicate accords for Sunday brunch.

Covid left 3 Black descendants
To care for angry hair
Without a mother
To share the bond
For every white father
Taken from a family
Able to access an army
Of fresh groceries
To compensate
For the misery of loss.

While those who live
In affection for one another
Must wait for a pox
To jump to lovers
Of different genders
Before power reveals the pathway
Of an adequate remedy to heal
A preventable affliction.

There is a cruelty
In your neglect
Of those you elect
To ignore for
Despite your poverty of consideration
We exist and would be you
If not for the luck
Of birth and affluent community.

For Us By Us

(Commissioned as Poetjournalist-in-Residence of The Rodham Institute)

Decades long
Draped in finery
With sensibility
We shape
The style of our identity
Better than others
Profit retired
Within the zip codes
Where streets
Parade our attire.

But when
Our most vulnerable
Seeking the expert design
Of health care to heal
The flesh that coats our bones
Wait times for procedures
Required to stitch
The fabric of elders
So they remain vibrant
Within community
Are longer than the time
Contemporary fashion trends
Have their relevance ebb
Like the coastal tide of doctors
Who long since deserted
The pavement of humanity
Where their capability
Is needed most.

Talent is no accident of birth
The skills required
to be human mechanics
For our streets
Are embodied in an apprentice
Trained to treat those
Who reside as neighbors.

A healthcare work force by us
Bringing wellness for us
In a way where
There is an authenticity
To the care
An onramp to the highway
Of prosperity
For our community.

East of the River

(Commissioned as Poetjournalist-in-Residence of The Rodham Institute)

Hewn trees give way to soil strewn lawns
Africa birthed by the Freedman's Bureau
In my land beside the Anacostia.

Tornados desolate homes and hurl buses
Drunken havoc that only the mental debris
East of the River in DC can better the instruction.

Gusts of air tear a community in two
But the wind from my lungs was
Sapped by decades of deteriorated air
And water cajoled from pipes
That leached the history of my people
into the marrow of my soul.

The food you gave me access to
Filled my arteries like the BMWs in standstill
Broadening the beltway at 8
Gazing at the slate of options on their phones
I tread down unlit sunset streets to stores
Where packages wrap the delicacies I shouldn't eat.

Two centuries of a system that kept me
On the sunrise side of a barricaded sea
The bedsprings of hate and intent to isolate
Gave way to the bureaucracy
That leads me from my lodgings.

But east of the river is my home
Even though I am distributed through a city
Where so many look like me but I am not home
Until lukewarm I return to construction dust
Beneath feet told to leave the land
Of my tobacco ancestry on the farm.

There is no guilt in my pride
At this altar of my past I am a muse
Amongst those of different caste
Who treat Barry as their home
But don't carry the burden of its antiquity
in their leathered bags or red-bottomed shoes.

I take kindly to the doctors who break from their kind
Whose borders are the tributaries
That separate wards and make us wards of a state
We want to adore.

The wellness they bring brews hope more than joy
And health that procures the years to reflect
That I might otherwise lose
So I thank them.

But my gratitude bleeds resentment
Where you perceive charity
I find the interest of an absent debtor
Owed to those East of the River.

A Shift Toward Justice

(Commissioned as Poetjournalist-in-Residence of Ovation TV)

Rodney Wilson's courage
Being authentic
His story shared
In the context of world wars
To students engaged
And informed but not swayed
As the naysayers
Would create stories of doomsdays
That never came
To take place.

His sensibility
In the face of fear
Generated a month
Of reflection
When so many find strength
to not just feel and know
But express
The identity that is their soul
Striving to exist in communities
That all too often resist
What they do not understand
But now more can
In a land where education stands
As the fortress against
The indignation of ignorance.

This month
Gives us a chance
To celebrate
Reflect
And bring the change
That frees us all
To live the year with
A shift toward justice
That makes us all
More whole
Than we were
Before.

Poverty of Compassion

(Commissioned as Poetjournalist-in-Residence of Ovation TV)

Martin Luther King
Spoke of the forgotten
Deprived of dignity
Trapped in despair
A web he fought
To untangle.

There is abundance today
A prosperity
Not known in history
A magnitude only surpassed
By the disdain
Dispassionate disposition
Of indifferent emotion
For those still hoping
To break the bonds
Of a system that makes the lottery
The game of the day.

His compassion
Is what I miss most
Despite a history
Where I remain optimistic
But it requires a care
Not found in a digital day
But perhaps a word, a note
Will compel us
To contemplate
The souls
That reside in others.

Garden of Brightmoor

(Commissioned as Poetjournalist-in-Residence of The Max M. and Marjorie S. Fisher Foundation)

Brown eyes inquiring
Beneath barely formed eyebrows
Winding to corkscrews of indelicate hair
Letting her know she must tend
To this emerging mind
Emanating from disregarded city streets
Forming broken tree limbs from last winter's storm
In the Garden of Brightmoor.

Homes stricken with the debris of racism
And decay of human compassion
Distract from determined women
Dedicated to caring for the next generation
In the Garden of Brightmoor.

Pierson street home to heroes
Licensed for 12 minds in diapers
Nurturing descendants
To the greatness of their capability
As consistent daily routines prepare them
To engage with the grace of family
What some see as care does not reflect
The borne weight of responsibility
And education that takes place
In the Garden of Brightmoor.

Concrete landscape where EBT replaces Apple Card
Buying necessities for the miniature kitchens
Tended to by heirs to inequality
Whose banks have shelves instead of tellers
And students focusing on basketball and screaming
With the joy they have for one another
If only the bus routes found their way to them
Like the loose parts play every morning
After picking weeds that look like flowers
In the Garden of Brightmoor.

Exquisite kinky hair cascading
Across the Grace Byers book saying
I am Enough with shoes shaped like animals
And fake ovens on floors baking memories
That last a millennia
In the Garden of Brightmoor.

Multicolored carpet strewn with toys
And hopes not yet realized
Under fluorescent lights casting shadows of opportunity
From open ceilings hewn with beams
Shielding an underserved future
And trees painted on walls with colors in the currency
Of calculated learning building a bridge
Beyond the blight to a prized space to be able to give back
To these matrons who gave so much
To make so many so much more
Than they would have been otherwise
In the Garden of Brightmoor.

They may not see the harvests of their labor
For the season it takes a woman
To build the future of who we are
Is longer than the time our vegetables and fruit
Are carted across the contours of a country
That leaves them just far enough away to ignore
Given what's stowed at my local store
Otherwise an easy choice for those who live
In a more desired zip code
But the children will reap what they have sowed
In the Garden of Brightmoor.

This is what they are planting
This is who they are tending
Detroit is where they are staying
This is why we should hear them
This is why we should adore them
Now is when they should be revered
In the Garden of Brightmoor.

Maternal Instincts

*(Commissioned as Poetjournalist-in-Residence of The Charles H. Wright
Museum of African American History)*

Carved from a past
Silhouetted with the women
Who etched their accomplishments
Into the fabric of a union
More perfect laced
With the instincts
Of mothers, daughters, and sisters
I am a whole
Otherwise unknown.

Sojourner casting truth
Into a pond filled with the injustice
Of forgotten wrongs
Harriet illuminating pathways
To a land promised but not yet realized
By those without hope
Found only through the light
Of a woman we take the time now
In these 31 days to commemorate.

Rosa taking a seat
So men could stand up strong
And follow in the footsteps
Of humble courage
Shirley Chisholm breaking boundaries
Beyond a movement of suffrage
To chisel a vote and voice
For those yet unheard
In the hallways on hills domed
With the iron fist of homogeneity.

A month is not enough
But I will strive
To better the instruction settled
Into my history by women
Whose remnants of solidarity
To an idea of equality
Echo in the opportunity
Available if my sons assemble
The ability to be worthy
Of their memory.

Refugee

Darya drags the Eagle Creek bag
Too large to be a carry-on on Delta
But the mosh pit journey she takes
Lacks the sounds of grunge rock
And grungy shoes on rock
Pass on the rhythm of her pulse which sounds
The pace of anxiety not spin class.

She gazes ahead through eyes amber
Not from biology but from the sun filtered
Through days, regrets and acne tears
And broken glasses hide the clarity
That no new home will spawn
Beyond the crest of the rubble-strewn hill
That now hides the coming dawn.

War doesn't just talk to the poor
Or take from those without
It found Darya before dance
Replacing Capezio shoes with the silhouette of pity
Illuminated by the cameras of CNN and charity
My donation comforts me.

Indigenous
(Commissioned as Poetjournalist-in-Residence of Ovation TV)

Beautiful

Serene
      Ostracized

Regal

Colorful
      Taken

Organized

Strategic
      Removed

Tenacious

Respectful
      Relocated

Harmonious

Natural
      Separated

Spiritual

Intellectual
      Mistreated

Physical

Artistic
      Massacred

Immortal

Still They Fight

Dignity defies the mothership
desecrating their land
As I cast an Ode to Angelou.

A mixed American standing in the shadows
While families squat homeless in subways
Yet have homes.

Resolute as they sit
Upon desks of annihilated steel
Hurling javelins at the iron gods of war they fight
Against fellow fathers and daughters' sons.

Grandmothers' insults slung on city streets
Dignified next to sarcasm-soaked words
Cloaking the iron missile meant for their sons' sons.

How do you break bread with those breaking bad?
Wheelchair stuck in the mud of war
Cratered in the memories of senseless loss
A child picks through the rubble of their mind
Orphaned by a soldiered father
And raped mother who is there but not still.

I would like to believe I would fight but would I?
My comfort steals away the strength
Of desperation and despair so I am left weak
But in awe and debt.

A superpower Uber ride rejected
For battle vests where comedy carved a path
To greatness. They still fight.

We fear battles on our shore so we feed them
Meals of anti-tanks and jets
So we don't have to as they fight still
Part of me envies the valor and beauty
Of human deeds in war.

My tour is interrupted by sales
Of soap and prescription drugs
That keep me clean of atrocities on my digital screens
So I can flip the switch as they still fight.

I dine wondering why the service is so slow
Post a pandemic as they fight still
I heckle political theatre and hang my head in shame
As a black man strikes a black man in a theatre but not for theatre
And yet it is theatre to us as they fight still.

I send money through the Etsy artist
Whose art comforts my walls and days
To fund his daily trek carting necessities and people instead of art
to the fight
Still they fight.

I thought Russians would make quick work
Of these metal workers and farmers
We all did 'cause we forgot the capacity of human spirit
When it is dispirited, they fight still.

In defeat still they are victorious
There is no amount of slaughter now
That will bring invaders victory
A people who thought they were free as their mayors stood on tanks
Now know they are not free as they slaughter mayors under tanks.

Still they fight
A people who knew they were free
Did not know how they could succeed
And love one another
So they fight.

Borders matter less
Than people who define a nation
They are Ukraine, still they fight.

In this moment I am Ukraine
Until the commercial break masks their pain
Still they fight.

I am with them in the best way
The uninvaded can maintain.

Still they fight
I feel my freedom in the coarseness
Of their struggle
Still they fight.

Their injustice is everywhere
Still they fight.

They fight still
For me.

Still they fight.

3
ON THE BLACK EXPERIENCE

Mahogany Stories

(Commissioned as Poetjournalist-in-Residence of The Charles H. Wright Museum of African American History)

Black and gold crown my entrance to
And Still We Rise at the Wright
Words of Maya Angelou echoing
With expectancy in the rotunda
Rocketing me through ancestry I feel
Yet do not know
Of these mahogany stories.

How can I feel the epic majesty
Of being African and in America
But not know the actuality
Of African royalty?

How is it I can feel the misery
Of a middle passage journey
But not know the authentic anguish
Of over 12 million crossing the Atlantic
To colonies not even countries already
Creating mahogany stories.

How is it I can feel the torment
Of ancestors enslaved
But dare not know the extent of children taken
And the documentation of humans standing
For sale in the public square?

How can I feel the righteousness
To stand up for what I believe
On a bus like Rosa
Or in the streets
But not know Ella Jo Baker
And so many who etched a path
Past 40 acres lost to treachery
So I can relive their travels today
In the form of mahogany stories?

How can I feel the fear
Of authority in my bones
Yet not know of the riots of 67
And that it was a rebellion?
How can I feel the heroes of Spike Lee
In films that tell my story
But not know Oscar Micheaux?
And how can I feel
What it is to be Detroit
Whether on Lafayette or a freeway
But not know Black Bottom as the birthplace
Of so many mahogany stories?

So I come to an exhibit
In this altar to my kin
Feasting on a banquet of knowing
The antiquity of my people that is pumping
Through my arteries every day fueling
What I have been feeling providing
Me the utility to elevate this sensibility
Into activities that transform the reality
Of my present that will be someone's history
One day walking through exhibits
Of my mahogany stories.

The Green Book

(Commissioned as Poetjournalist-in-Residence of The Charles H. Wright Museum of African American History)

Standing as a figurine
Of my Negro roots
And American experience
Guide to injustice
Victor Green drafted a manual
For my forebears
Saving as many lives
As a ban on minty nicotine
Would if it could
Today.

Kerosene illuminating
The lighter side
Of discrimination
Radar for a family
Of my blood
Beacon to a place
To break bread, be entertained
Architect the hair of the day
Fueling the automobile
Providing freedom
Vaccine to the daily grind
Of segregation.

I take for granted the hotel
Found on an app
That doesn't take my color into account
And the restaurant selected from reviews
Based on the character of culinary ingredients
Instead of the content of my melanin.

A time not long ago
Gleaned from this tome
for black Americans
To find a safe space
When a place on the road
Filled with hatred seemed something
Far beyond the inability to thrive.

There is a glimmer of hope
In the distance my nation has traveled
Down this road since the book
Dreamed of a day when equality
Simmering at southern rest stops
Would mean anyone could go
And be seen where they please.

But I find relics of times thought past
In the million miles I have driven
Without the Green Book as my escort
That provide a scenic index to my times
Bringing me to wonder what book
My grandchildren will need
With urgency.

Pulse of My People

*(Commissioned as Poetjournalist-in-Residence of The Charles H. Wright
Museum of African American History)*

Cement carves a path
Piercing city blocks that separate me
From the plaza of my people.

Silhouetted streetlights illuminate
The sinewy bodies of my textured kin
And celebration of the Sphinx
As I cross the barricades
Stepping onto the concrete playground
As the Detroit River reverberates
The rhythm of Africa across this urban canvas
An anchor for my blackness.

Between ebony legs
The drum is just an extension of lungs
Breathing billows of sound that traveled through history
To envelop me this side of Jefferson
An avenue to cross, not a president
Whose democracy cradles me
In shadows of slave ancestry.

An obsidian dancer's back arches
Between ambient sun and spherical streetlamps
Shrouding the brick paver that bears the weight
Born by her daily diary
Declared through stretched muscles
That invite me to share her jubilance of this juncture
In time.

We share
And I share in the burden of my people.

Brown eyes reflect yellow and blue finery
Celebrating a history that brings dignity
Despite an undignified crossing
I see truth with my city mirrored
In the faces of mingled children
Unbridled in youth

Fueled by who they are
And who they are born to be
And not yet assigned to be
By a country not yet ready
For their ferocious hair that sows
The passion of my people
For we are Pharaohs.

I stride on
As the pain in my lower back
Retained from the factory floor
Is subdued by pride
And melodies of Jollof rice and fufu
Mate with bowls of harissa and injera bread
As they undulate through melanin
And the arteries of my soul.

These contemporary hieroglyphs
A roadmap to 3000 years of legacy
Constructing cliffs of identity
Driving me every day
to be me.

I am agile, I am awash
Reasoned yet artful
Thoughtful yet passioned
In this
The pulse of my people.

A Pryor Love

(Commissioned as Poetjournalist-in-Residence of The Charles H. Wright Museum of African American History)

Quiet power
Formed and projected
The soulful sturdiness
Of matrons cemented in history
Beacons of strength and ability
Born from circumstance
And faith in future generations.

Josephine a violin soloist
Commanded a piano
An accompanist on the stage of life
With music and a lover lost
Taking performance to education
With a studio the bridge
Inspired by seeing her people
Represented in literature
The way she saw herself
In the mirror every day.

Dell the caregiver developed
From the integrity of a city
Nurtured in spaces
Where dance and marksmanship
Define the direction
Of design and creativity.

Both extraordinary women
With inspiration birthed
From the pain of lost companions
That gave leaders clarity
For a House of Heritage
And Cluttered Corners.

To whom much is given
Borne is a weight
Of expectation upon which
They bettered the instruction
Earning so much more
Crushing barriers
Not just for themselves
But for all of Detroit
And all of us
Paving a way
That built the bedrock
Upon which my words
Could not be constructed
So I celebrate a century
Of their contributions
To our community.

Negro

I am a Negro.

Don't a Negro got eyes? Don't a Negro got skin?
Don't a Negro got ears which can be boxed?
Don't a Negro got a tongue with which to spit forth words,
   a brow upon which sweat can build,
    a stomach which can be robbed of sweet nutrients?
Don't a Negro got an ego to be bruised, pride to muster?

Tempted by similar sin, emboldened by like religions,
   enticed by the same sugarcane.
If you crack a whip upon our backs
   do we not bleed?

If you take our daughters from us
   before dawn do we not suffer defeat?
If you stick us with a needle
   don't we get high?
If you terminate our leaders
   do we not rise up?

If a Negro stand tall,
   why must it be a ball in his hand?
A white man can hold a pen, white women
   can gather and share their stories.

If you feed us with cheese manufactured
   by you, will we not eat and learn
    not how to plant our own seed?

If you clothe our backs
   and shelter us from the elements,
      shall we not yearn to avoid work
         in the sweltering sun?
You have had the seasons to change,
   however you choose to stagnate.
I can't allow this type of justice
   to remain.

Don't you got eyes that you're tinting with contacts?
Don't you got skin you're coating with animal's oil?
Don't you got a tongue you're usin'
   to talk like an urban historian?
Don't you got ears that want to hear
   the beat of a Negro drum?

The verbal jibes which you have thrown,
   I can accept when I see
      how you treat your own.

Don't forget where that darker shade
   of pale came from,
Don't you recognize our ancestors'
   bootleg lovin'?

I'm glad you were the one
   who invented the mirror.
I'll use it whenever you want me
   to forget what I remember...

Aren't you a Negro too?

The Sound of Martin Luther King

(Commissioned as Poetjournalist-in-Residence of The Charles H. Wright Museum of African American History)

I hear you
Standing for what was right
I see your words
Beyond the grave
Lulling my child to sleep
After a day of injustice.

I feel your dream
While cloaked amidst
Hate and segregation
Still found
Despite the rights
And justice you prevailed
For a time.

I find your legacy
Is found in my life filled
With better mornings
Than my father or his father
Whose blood comprised
Of your struggle
Stand before me so
I have an equality
They did not
Even though
I am not equal yet.

I take this day
Your day to look back
While moving ahead
With a message bred
Into the melanin of my soul
Thankful for your dream
A reality
I get to live
Imperfectly
Today.

28 Days

(Commissioned as Poetjournalist-in-Residence of The Rodham Institute)

Brought in chains
On ships of shame
A stolen people, renamed
But still we rise, over time
Spirited.

Black history
Stories of glory and pain
Told in this shortest month
Share the struggle and resistance
Of a people strong.

Freedom echoes
In the songs
From fields of cotton
To streets of hate
As memories dissipate for those
Who didn't need to walk tall
Waiting for a seat earned.

Firehoses and dogs
Flanked the billy clubs
That failed to defeat
Marches and speeches
Built from a bravery
I do not have the experiences
To generate.

Lineage of a people
Unbroken like the shackles that remain
Comprised of poverty and inequality
Instead of iron cast in a history
Darkened by those enlightened
With bigotry and fear.

From slavery to civil rights
Segregation, discrimination
Confronted with determination
I speak with reflection and honor
Striving for a future
Where those from my blood line
Will speak of this month of history
Differently.

MLK Day
(Commissioned as Poetjournalist-in-Residence of The Rodham Institute)

A moment to reflect
On one who fought
For a dream of wellness
For all shades of humanity.

We are a tale of two cities
A nation dispersed
Within another
Realities seen
In doctors and wait times
And those who have to price out medicine
Like supermarket isles
Seeking a bargain
In the moment
Finding the price paid
Is far more harsh
In the winter of our time.

He saw the inequality
And built a stage
Upon which
We can all perform
But who are the players
In this story
Of privilege and disparity?

I find myself unequal
To the history
That built opportunities for me
So I pause
In this moment
To find the strength
To be better
For others
Than me.

Obama

(Commissioned as Poetjournalist-in-Residence of The Charles H. Wright Museum of African American History)

I did not think you could win

My afro grabbed from behind
In high school before German class
The country I grew up in
Told me a man named Hussein
Could not take the reins of a nation
Not yet ready for your immensity.

I did not think you could win.

Despite your striking features
chiseled stature with soft eyes
conveying a confidence of ability
sustained by wit, intellect
And ethics of work and family
The people I grew up with
Would let Kenyan biology
Drive their vote more than
Kansas maternity that together define
Not only you but a society
Not yet ready for your identity.

I did not think you could win.

But a passion overtook me
To try to be a part
Of a history
I could not see
But believed in so I strived
With the first arts policy committee
To be part of the stage of a candidacy
For a presidency that could redefine
My history fabricating a future I did not think
A people were ready for.

But they were
And you did
Win.

We
Did win.

And now I believe in things
Never part of my saga
Because I find myself
In a domain where the sphere
Of possibility is defined by pioneers
Like Barack Hussein Obama.

First Fruit

(Commissioned as Poetjournalist-in-Residence of The Charles H. Wright Museum of African American History)

Origins lie in harvests
Of a motherland
Fields of history fill
Ancestral baskets
Of pride, theft
And passion for my people.

My nation now
Built upon the weight
Of uncompensated labor
And love for an ideal
Not yet realized in a place
Where we strive for a more perfect
Space to raise the future
With whom we now celebrate
This holiday.

Colors in a candelabra
Made of the metal
Of bruised immortality
Cast shadows of Black, red, and green
Silhouetting the painful past
Of struggle from pastures of hope
Reflected in the blackness
Conjured in my mirror every morning.

Unity of disparate cultures
Connect a continent of shared experience
Leading to self-determination
Comprised of collective work
And responsibility.

Where the path
To a prosperity earned
But not yet seen
Requires cooperative economics
Driven by purpose
Fueled with the sheer creativity
Of poets and engineers.

As I gaze at my mother I never knew
Til the age of 31 brought her love
Of my memory into reality
As a reunification of family
Giving me faith fulfilling a mantra
Reflected in this moment
Not just for my kin
But for the saga of my people
Whose journey is captured
In these precious days
Of Kwanzaa.

The Boy King

(Commissioned as Poetjournalist-in-Residence of The Charles H. Wright Museum of African American History)

His oval orbs penetrate my persecuted soul
Traversing the gift of the Nile and Common Era
Emptying into the Mediterranean Sea
Of my pride.

He didn't live as long as I have
But he lived more as I long to
He gave belief in the many
Back to the many
Defying a father deceased
Like the carnage of my family
As I seek identity in his image.

I thought myself descended from slaves
Til his golden gaze gave me a more learned way
To glimpse in the mirror every morning
As I cleanse my teeth from nightmares
Of inequality.

Glass and gemstones adorn
The lapis lazuli that frame
Quartz eyes with obsidian that beckon me
To be honored ancestry
And take stock of a life of royalty
That diverges from my daily strife.

A narrow beard of blue and gold
Disarming my fear of failure
While kneeling before the vulture
And his cobra crown I rise
To bring a noble nature to my offspring
My Egyptian essence overwhelming.

These artifacts merely historical healing
I stand in awe of their majesty
Mooring me to a lineage bearing the brown sheathing
Emboldening my courage to advocate
For my community.

The moment fleeting
Retreating I am reborn
From ancient history
A cacophony of boldness rising.

A sampling scroll of the surging
Strength within my scaffolding
I am whole
I am the boy king.

Espresso

Nothing's simple nowadays
    Information highways and banking to go,
There was a time when
    Simplicity was sublime,
Music and people, Black or white
    Contrasting, lines of sight.
You take your caffé latte, I'll have espresso.

Like a backhoe in my spice garden
    of turmeric and oregano,
Inferring political shame
    Diversity calls my name,
Only biological parentage
    to blame.
You take your caffé latte, I'll have espresso.

Where's my charcoal pick with fist,
    my matted afro?
Taken like Sanford and Son,
    George Jefferson,
There's still Hughley, Tommy D, Keenan Ivory
    Who's runnin' the WB?
You take your caffé latte, I'll have espresso.

So I'm mixed,
    Mulatto hypocrite, I know,
Although I complained, most things remain the same,
    What's to gain?
Senate's still pasteurized, prison just homogenized,
    with separatism prized.
You take your caffé latte, I'll have espresso.

I think they lied, 'cause the chasm's just as wide,
    We never really tried Jim Crow,
HBCU's and the UNCF
    mean the ACLU ain't got a clue,
With BET and the NAACP,
    who needs a unity?
You take your caffé latte, I'll have espresso.

I know there's ebony in my eye
    and calcium in my marrow,
But multi-cultural is taxing,
    this onyx floor don't need waxin',
Why not let me pay and have my say
    I'm lactose intolerant anyway.
You take your caffé latte,
I'll have espresso.

ON MY IDENTITY

4

They Said I Wasn't Really Black

Born from white and brown young skins,
I was so diff'rent from the pack.
Adopted by Caucasians at just 2 weeks of age,
They couldn't have known about the other people;
They said I wasn't really Black.

A violinist I was destined for,
Early on I showed them the knack.
It was Mozart for me and Beethoven too,
I never got to memorize Jackson 5 lyrics so;
They said I wasn't really Black.

School bells and cafeteria food,
I sat there with my brown lunch sack.
There was no fried chicken in my zip-lock bag,
No confrontation between watermelon and black-eyed peas;
They said I wasn't really Black.

I'd stroll into the rehearsal room
Wishing I was the Daddy-Mack.
I didn't even go to the games, let alone sport the jersey,
Hell, I wasn't even in the band and I wonder why;
They said I wasn't really Black.

I didn't talk the talk and couldn't walk the walk,
Familial prec'dent I did lack.
At first it seemed correct by design,
It took me years 'til I was uncomfortable when;
They said I wasn't really Black.

There were those who made me feel different,
And few who I thought had my back.
I could have taken all the racial slurs
If only it wasn't my friends around when;
They said I wasn't really Black.

All I sought was acceptance,
Any clique's shell I could not crack.
They feared the anomaly, too bad for me,
That I got good grades, couldn't play spades 'cause;
They said I wasn't really Black.

Then it settled down on me,
Weighting unease upon my back.
Like the line and rhyme of these words I write,
I had only just begun to fight when;
They said I wasn't really Black.

The first African Queen I was to know
Drew me in like the sweet lilac.
She shut those doors, supposedly wanted more,
But I knew the reason behind because;
They said I wasn't really Black.

For a time I had an Afro,
It should have got me on the track.
Foolish me, to think they'd see, what I wanted to be.
Why did they all have to agree?
My skin was just a racial gi. Hopelessly, eventually;
They said I wasn't really Black.

I'm glad I found out that they were wrong,
I ain't born in Uncle Tom's shack!
I guess they wish that color was not what it is,
But what they wanted it to be when;
They said I wasn't really Black.

I have come to terms with what I cannot fight
I yearn no longer to attack.
The title I sought without emerged from within.
There was serenity in complacency when imperious to chagrin while;
They said I wasn't really Black.

Every moment I burst with pride,
I toss a memory in my sack.
Their jibes ebb like the tide, as I open the floodgates wide,
It was quite a ride,
Over now save the rare aside, I wish I wouldn't have cried,
I kinda hope they lied when;
They said I wasn't really Black.

Nigel

Black
as a desert night.
Friend
always around to refund problems.
Wish
my color was as simple as his.
You
ridiculed our bond.
Were
my spirit to fall, he would catch it.
Here,
he'd say, returning it emboldened.
I
shared my bed with him 'til I was ten.
Love
remembering that look in his eyes.
You
came only close to knowing my cat.

Picture Perfect

Picture perfect,
It took your death for me
To realize how perfect
You really are.

Violin lessons,
You took from me the hate
I had for you for making me
Do things that gave me life lessons.

You loved how much I loved another
And how you knew I needed
What I knew wasn't needed but now I do...
But now I do.

And it's too late to tell you
But I said enough for you to know, before you died.
Since I was a child I never lied to you I fear
I didn't try enough.

To share the truth of my life
And now I know you better than I did
When you were alive and I want to try harder
But why?

When Dad scattered your ashes
The sky in the backyard turned to music
And I heard your hair whistle
Through the evergreens and Dad's tears.
. . . and we stood there . . .

And maybe it's not right but
I'm mad at you again, I see
Ten or more years of his life without you
Looking at him and I can't bear the pain.

I've only got years of love to gain,
I'm just a child but he's taken the train.
I know you made it easy on us but
If you would have made it harder, it'd be easier now.

And Dad loves you more than I do
Which is more than I did before
So I weep for him
Because it's easier.

But I don't want things easier
Because I need to earn the pain of your loss
And you are in most things of my day
So I move on.

And make them mine again
And then I see you
And you'll be there...
Today... in May.

You will be there and all that I am
That is owed to you is finally a part of me with you
So you're in the backyard and in my violin
And in my son's eyes and Dad's tears.

And, I love the things I do
Everyday
With you
Still.

Picture perfect.

Gram

The following words
      fall short
Of your stature.

Double chocolate chip
      cookies in the summertime,
Visiting you in June,
      remembering when I flew.

The boots you picked out
      for me to ride Sparky,
Dusty sparse mountain trails by your house.

Monopoly best started before
      the four to five o'clock kids' hour,
In the pool.

Real estate consolidation over chlorine,
      Starsky and Hutch so cool,
With no TV back home.

Wish mom didn't have to bring you
      here last year,
Easier to say farewell,

If they had let you die,
      less time to cry, it's nice,
Playing my violin for you still.

We're stuck in the same old timeline,
        you get to jump around, free,
Do as you please.

I love that when you see my mother
        as a little girl,
You smile.

Your twenty-dollar birthday card
        was my family when they weren't,
Worst of early adult rebellion.

I know you're not really there,
        already begun to travel,
I see your little visits,

When I perform
        William Grant Still,
For you.

Thanks for the look last time,
        I was with your body at the home,
Meant the world to me.

Should have said goodbye already,
        you know I'm still checkin' in,
When I fall asleep.

You let your body return
        to where it was forged, then,
I'll tip my cap and bid you adieu.

The Road Not Taken
(inspired by Robert Frost)

Two choices lay before my solemn eyes
As if two roads beneath my cleat
Where laughter diverged from impatient cries
And trust unfound in deep disguise
While love endured as noble feat.

To leave seemed safe, a neat design
To stay brought comfort, warm embrace
I chose the latter upon to dine
Perhaps a choice not even mine
For both that day were equal place.

One path had trodden black upon me
One path could have shed new light
Bad memories find a way to flee
Compromised by the joys set free
Releasing me the will to fight.

Wisdom I will one day share
With shadowed tongue or cursive pen
I knew the path with lesser wear
But inside truth was laid out bare
And I thought I loved you then.

My First Teacher

Mr. Graffman was old,
Russian immigrant.

His apartment was brown, I remember,
I was only seven, it was East Side, mid-town.
He'd always say, you no talk you play.

He was dedicated
With my talent evident.

He would sit at the big black grand piano,
Ejecting praise, criticism like a little Hobbit,
I'd correct the mistakes quickly, muttering,
He would question my practice hours sincerity.
He'd always say, you no talk you play.

I was Black,
Boy, that was different.

After Lalo was concluded, his offerings complete
Anguishing, I gauged his satisfaction,
                    rarely recognizing his mood.
Passing the bar meant one of those candies, my pick of color even,
From that crystal jar sparkling on the side table, oasis
                    amongst the Earthen tapestries.
He'd always say, you no talk you play.

I'd loosen my bow, pack my violin,
Music and sugar succulent.

More often than not, savoring,
       I'd return home with orange tongue,
               my favorite flavor.
Sliding the rickety gate shut,
     as I pulled the elevator lever,
     always returning to the lobby late.
That ride almost as fun as the Bartok duets;
     There was no practice time to prepare
              for when he died.

That time I would have complied.
He'd always say, you no talk you play.

Stealing 20s

Mom's purse carried
so many twenties
every two weeks.

Don't really know how
but I found that out;
wish I hadn't.

I had no toys
they didn't support
mindless action.

I got no sweets
such simple pleasures
were deemed bad food.

Just some Legos
not even shaped ones
plain building blocks.

If only there had been
something other than
books, practicing.

With so many
would a few be missed?
All those twenties.

I did it once
breathless, waiting for
the belt to come.

I bought Twinkies,
gum and Suzy-Qs,
hot fudge sundaes.

Ate like a prince,
too bad it lasted
only two weeks.

Didn't get caught
could I not repeat
what satisfied me?

They were asleep;
my moral compass
was asleep.

Kingly dining
accompanied by
ten Matchbox cars.

The joy of toys
cut short by fury.
They knew, of course.

Tried the window
but Dad saw their flight
to the cement.

Leather found my
flesh more times than I
can remember.

Glad I grew up,
found my principles
before prison.

Wish I knew then
how much I hurt them
while learning trust.

Where was my head
I never steal now
in poverty.

Whip my boy, too
to teach the lesson
if he's like me.

Dachau

Ovens still smoldering
under the August sun.
I thought I saw a bone,
thirteen-year-old trav'ler,
How could I be the son of Jews?

Chilled by my sweating neck,
gravel crunching, beneath
feet accustomed to streets,
descend to the showers.
What possessed them to go willing?

Slaves had the whip and chains.
I understand why most
would not revolt, but Death?
Why? They shared a color,
Reprimand for a religion?

Mom and Dad don't believe.
Gestapo soldiers would
Slaughter them anyway.
Fear! Would they have chosen me,
Even though I was adopted?

Exhibition pictures,
medical, altitude,
low-cost experiments.
Every one bore my face.
Mood transfixed if it could be me.

Prior to awareness,
it was just my Blackness,
now a Reich hated me.
Why won't someone tell them?
More enemies, less friends to trust.

Relief showered, tour done.
Beyond the earthen pits,
fossils of passive men
Led past broken barbed wire.
Angry, why didn't they struggle?

That wretched history,
allowed wrong,
hope at home.

Some white people suffered,
ancestors understand.
What!

Jews and Blacks don't get along?

The Coming

Mute rupturing,
while eating Puerto Rican food.

Meeting by the meter
'cause the bill took too long
to pay by credit card.

Navigating,
through heavy breathing signal lights.

Parking where the permit
allows, by the wheelchairs
and automatic doors.

Mucous gushing,
car door opening too slow.

As I help her, help him.
Elevator rising,
the maternity ward.

Nurse admitting,
Never noticing she was fine.

Luxury perceptions,
mass depreciating.
Genes recalibrated.

Exercising,
now forbidden planning, damn breach.

Nine hours plus noon signaled
only the beginning
method of measurement.

Pain increasing,
six hours dilating, no progress.

Begone natural birth,
her eyes, genuflecting.
I ordered the morphine.

Five hours tasking,
fear earning five centimeters

Pride disintegrating,
frustrating the birth plan,
bidding anesthesia.

Percolating,
my wife's collecting stamina.

Ten hours contemplating,
contempt resonating
for unrepenting staff.

Undulating,
twenty-two expecting hours plus.

Repetitious pushing,
his crowning commencing,
will capitulating.

Representing
blackness reciprocating white.

Head regurgitating,
gesticulating hands
conjugating, he comes.

Music of You

Ringing in my head
Composers living closer than Beethoven
Sitting in studio class
I listened to your love.

Of music I knew
Nothing of the dead men who colored the mask
You wore protecting strangers
From knowing you within.

The imperfect hair
Interlocking, cascading, encircling,
The truth was I did not yet
Love you in that way.

In the way that words
Can ring true to those who wander in heather
But the key in Ysaÿe
Changes like butterflies.

Then I was alone,
For long enough for people but not enough
To know that on bended knee
Left skinned, scabbed and bleeding.

The cacophony
Of Ysaÿe, I wanted sonority
Melody to shower me
Replace delicacy.

I threw the symbol
Of what I knew I needed but did not need
Because melody does not
Suit me one little bit.

The music of you
Dresses me every day in a way that draws
My mother's breath through Dad's tears
And wilted evergreens.

The ringing did stop
Once my finger felt the ring whose time was wrong
But wasn't and I know
Now what I knew then.

You are in my life
My violin carries your soul through Noah's voice
Your dress colors the backyard
In Asian Spring tears

I shed tears for your
Tears you shed for me for the tears my Dad fails
To shed for me once before
Or now from afar.

And Sue was right,
The ring brings the music of my life through
Reviving the truth that I
Love that I love you.

Garage Cigarette

Smoke fills the openness and tool shelf
with cars sitting cold
Warming the space between
Jousif and myself

Coldness fills the distance
Of cultures and geography
Icicles of disdain for Americana and divorce
Serving as a true love's resistance.

Maybe even color played a part,
But did it really matter?
A cognac cat smoothed our breath
As we spoke of the love I had to impart.

For a woman, and even though I thought her nation
Treated her as a daughter, she was a daughter
So, respect was due to parents responsible
For such an incredible creation.

We breathed the same air of cognac smoke and casino players
I came to know the man who was smart enough
To doubt that my love would endure but smarter still
To see the loyalty that lay beneath layers

Of Americana and divorce and still glimpses
Of the face of family that would be near
And share the humor of shallow care
And countrymen with empty promises.

Filling the fear of the inevitable, resignation
But knowing the legacy would be revered,
And Alexander would carry the memory
Through casinos and mockeries of society.

I am comforted by the infrequency
Of the rose petal voice that brings a decency
A decorum to his tragedy with a loyalty
That inspires me to follow her legacy.

And love her daughter not as I would have
Or as my mother loved me but as she loved he
For Rosa's love personifies an integrity
That only death can truly define.

I knew him as we smoked in the garage but didn't know
What he already knew,
That family trumped all else and, in the end,
I was to be part of what he had determined.

And making sure that of all the fears
For a father, the fear for his daughter
Could be passed on
to another.

And the sense of him for who he was
And how he met life's lessons
And how he filled the lifetimes of those who carry on
Would be treasured still, forever more
By those who loved his presence.

Nugget

It's like the miners
during the rush for gold
in the West.

Not the first ones,
ones who found something, built a life,
Not the ones after them, who built the bars and inns,
Not even the ones after them, who worked for them.

Rather the ones who read,
in the papers, months after,
All the main veins in the mountains,
shucked from the Earth's quarried grip.

The ones who got there last
whose desperate search
not for all the riches, to be found
but one golden nugget.

To give them hope,
to give them reason
for the months-long Conestoga
wagon travel.

To give reason for the dirt,
grime, flaking, off of eyebrows,
scent coming from folds in torn bodies,
Something to hold onto, companion,
in the midst of our palms.

A golden kernel,
true value not met,
by the six pence given
after weighed by the ornery barkeep.

That is what I ache for,
holding on, to give meaning,
finding my way,
so I can stay with my wife.

Baby Next Door

Intravenous tentacles
        protruding from beneath
Sterile Muppet sheets.

Light scarce through hospital gowns
        reflecting IV bags
soiled linen carts.

Preemies get their air through tubes
        Anne Geddes should put that
On a calendar.

No one to care that the chair
        becomes a make-shift cot,
Someone is to blame.

I don't often see color
        but his blackness fills me,
My people's madness!

Nurse Carol, his current Mom
        'til her shift is over
Good for six hours.

Lungs not yet developed give
        a kitten's cry for milk
Lulling us to sleep.

Only his heart monitor
            alarm would disturb us
Before a nurse came.

What kind of Mom with no Dad
            leaves a fatherless son
Two months out of nine?

Curtain protecting the sight
            of hearing his gurgles
And lapse of breathing.

Hooked up two weeks for each day
            Baby Noah had us,
Still there when we left.

I wonder if Mom or Dad
            wherever they may be
Feel quite so alone.

I hope I would be better
            if I put their shoes on,
They're nothing like me.

As we left him to his plight
            I felt sad yet I was
Glad, he wasn't mine.

The Waiting Room

The walls surrounding me are so spartan
But with art that's so safe that I don't think that is what art is for
But yet it makes me feel so safe
So maybe the time for art is not while I am here, waiting.

And, there's something about the food that's bad for you
In hospitals where you go when you eat food that is bad for you.
The irony does not escape me as I contemplate escaping
The waiting room to abate my nerves as I wish I wasn't here.

It begins with that first comment of concern
That sounds so benign through a doctor's voice who sees the signs,
Yet by design I find myself less curious
To know more about what could make my life less without her.

And so your heart which was beating the whole time
Becomes a more present pounding as I press down inside
So she assumes the calm of my serenity
As they ask me to wait in the waiting room outside.

But then she comes and I have known her well enough to know
That words unheard, reports unseen conveys the clean results to me
So we selfishly embrace as others still sit, life paused
I contemplate the cause with which we get to leave.

It is time again for the waiting room
But now I am in the gown; tilted down
As they bring their sense of the world
Inside me to find what they fear
So I fear as much as the sedation will permit me.

As I ponder that I am in here restless and she is out there waiting,
Thus, I am wishing I was there with her
In the room, waiting.

On anyone other than us.

My Birmingham Belle

Crowded halls filled with the sounds of students
Fighting for the class they need while calling to register;
Where was the technology then that lets them just go online now?
Lost in the halls with papers draping off of corkboard
like an opening curtain to an opera not yet written.

I get lost in the monotony of touchtones telling me my class is not available
not even a cog in a wheelwhich has purpose, I am lost,
my music lost in the tones of my wretched phone,
my money lost in the tomes of a forsaken bank
that says I am insufficient.

I walk down the tickertape hallway to the office
that those who made me feel lost said was a place.
A place they don't understand, I think,
because to this day, they have let the magic slip
and they have the power, the bank knows
they are sufficient enough to make a difference
to those who are lost and now I am lost again.

An oasis seems like an analogy but desert touches
on the shore of the saintly water upon which the thirsty traveler feasts
but the crowded sounds and crackle of paper and registrants
faded to black as I entered and saw her blackness.

I don't always see our color first but when whitewashed
in the sea of Maize and Blue tumbling into shore I do
Terrified of the undertow seeking to pull me out,
her overture to the opera of my life
was draped in the color of who she was.

Those who don't know would think I mean the color of her skin
but skin is only the flesh which changes with the changing sun,
roots are far darker and bear the sweetness of the fruit.
Her blackness came from Birmingham, it came from the source
of Martin's letter from the jail where he sojourned and she sojourned north
to bring her roots to the Maize and Blue.

Her sweetness came from her care, she was not soft with me,
her softness came from her care and in that moment I knew
I could find a way in this place; that there was torchlight
and when the going got tough and it did as one would expect
from the crowded hallways; she was there...
I went when I needed something and she delivered
but then I found myself there when I needed... nothing...
but drawn still to be even if just to sit for a time... with her.
And with others, I found a kinship, not in music...
not even in the music, but in our shared sense of her.

And she was as stern with me as she was with others on behalf of me
and when I mistook her love for equity, I called her Faye
upon which she schooled me that a Southern Belle
whose tenure at the Maize and Blue began before my heartbeat beat
was not equal and not just in years but in her care
and love for those who came before me.

I loved her for her love; for her reality which broke upon me
what it means to be cared for in a way that is real and now
as I speak to those grown as one who is grown, I realize
that there will never be a time when I may call her Faye
for I can never be her equal and as her heart now is still
and in a place where all must go, I love the dignity with which she carries
my memory of her forward as the first Southern Belle I was to know.

And as her bell tolls the song of Martin Luther King I think of how he knew
the great tragedy of our times was the silence of so many
in the face of challenge and injustice
and I am warmed by the voice of this Birmingham Belle
whose voice carried and created change; our seats changed; and now,
her voice speaks through those whom she has touched...
they speak through the teaching of a LaTonya Woods,
the baton of a Damon Gupton, the strings of a Tami Lee, the keys of a Karen
Walwyn,
the voices of a Louise Toppin, Karen Johnson, Brenda Wimberly
and so many others who could be named.

And now, to our Birmingham sage I tell, in the serenity and quiet
of this lovely place, touch the depths of truth, feel the hem of Heaven. You go
away well with old, good friends. And don't forget when you leave...
why you came, Mrs. Burton
Our sweet Southern Belle.

The Holidays
(Commissioned as Poetjournalist-in-Residence of Ovation TV)

Bittersweet chocolate
Baked in ovens
Breeds kinship
Between others
Brethren in a time
Bereft of dissonance.

Pastels evolved through seasons
Painted in red and green
Purposefully connecting
Parents and offspring disconnected
Parties drunk with lost emotion.

Digesting sugar, salt and fat
Driven by religion or emotion
Divested from intellect
Dabbling with lavish sin
Doused with charity
Divine I cherish.

The Holidays.

5

ON THE ARTS

Ovation

(Commissioned as Poetjournalist-in-Residence of Ovation TV)

Immaculate joy cascades from Coretta Scott's face
Arched over Martin, Yolanda and Martin Luther
Their fingers entangled with the ebony and ivory
Keys to a future seeking the harmony
They found in pews and the piano bench
In the salon on Sunset Avenue.

The notorious intellect of RBG
And arched eyebrows of Scalia
Disintegrate from decrees to wit
And gentle froth of friendship
Married by the arts
And brinkmanship of Figaro.

The heritage of who we are
Falls within the notes
Stanzas, pigments and strokes
As Lyndon boldly guides our inner vision
Revealing collective humanity.

When we speak and listen
Through creativity instead of
Tropes wreaked with rhetoric
Driven by fear encased in armor
Compromise arises that is not unity
Yet the hate subsides to indifference
To difference with each other.

Like Maya still I rise and call out
To state the character
Of my state lies not in doubt
When scrawled art of children
Still fills our tenement halls.

I need to claim if it please
The court of state
That art is the plate
Upon which we all
Dine the same.

A beltway world of screens
I sit still before a ballet of stories
Of those peculiar to me
Woven through silicon and pixels in 4k.

When the costumed aria ends
When the toe shoe returns to Marley floor
When the mystery confounds as it intends
When the Maestro's baton soars.

I stand.

Not in a hall of thousands
But alone in my ordinary room
I rise for this extraordinary fusion
These artists creating the cannon
Of an engine where we deepen
Our best selves woken.

A notion of who we are
I stand in Ovation.

Rise

Eight years before my birth
This hallowed hall trembled with the strains
Of a Black man's violin whose resonance waned
Too soon for too many who do not know
The name Sanford Allen
And the same is certain for me
And ultimately you as such is the lesson of memory
And history without which we would not be.

But this music brings immortality
To composers and creators
Capturing a reality of the lives we lead.

A rebel violinist destined for desertion
There was a lack of family for me
Byproduct of adoption and reunification
where you remain
The ancillary additive
Of a blended family.

My community was built by those
Whose identity graced stages
And delivered an attachment unconditional
Beyond the art we make
And lives we urgently transform.

I took a step and planted the seed
To bring a permanency
To this delicate discipline
That defines our human condition.

In the end a movement
Constituted from ingredients
Of talent and noble ambition
For which my greatest contribution
Was merely its inception.

Afa has taken Sphinx so far
Past its creation and each of them
So much more than I ever was
And yet I am so much more because of them
So I am filled with obligation grown
From the Virtuosi's devotion of practice
And craft pursued with courage
To take the stage that wasn't built for them
Yet now they call their own.

And Tommy Mesa's sonorous cello
Solicits strength as battles still lie ahead
For the incomplete story of our artform
Is yet to be penned
And I may not get there with you
My friend, like Martin I see the land of promise
We will realize in the harmonies
Manifested by Jessie Montgomery.

In genuflection, like Angelou I rise.
In ovation to them I rise
To what they convey
With creative cultural fusion.

Xavier Foley's fingers bearing notes
Expelled from a principled soul
To the musical page
I rise.

Amaryn Olmeda's melodies an aural turbulence
Echoing my children's laughter in the morning
So I rise.

Carlos Simon's chordal remedies
Restoring a democracy diminished
Within audiences of diversity
As I rise.

Rubén Rengel's regal virtuosity
Rendering an awe of immensity for the rigor required
Gaining a perfection within a discipline of complexity
I never attained
I rise.

Steadied by the E-string of Hannah White
Allowing hope spilling
Across my furrowed brow
From the tragedies of the day
Compelling me to rise.

As my founding vision is traced
By Valerie Coleman's victorious voice
Depicting our peoples' protection for our youth
In a world of dereliction
In recognition
I rise.

I rise Joseph Conyers
for your compassion of sound
Enveloping me with a profound character
And capacity for greatness and generosity.
I rise.

I rise for their fearlessness
I rise for their black and brownness.
I rise for their boundless intensity
I rise for my soul renewed
I rise for La Familia this Sphinx family
In Gratitude... I rise.

The Arts

*(Commissioned as Poetjournalist-in-Residence of The Max M. and Marjorie
S. Fisher Foundation)*

Scraps otherwise cast
Aside by society
Repurposed with intent
Become prisms
Of balance transforming
Our progeny's perspective
On a world of disarray
In adolescence.

The technique through which
Bodies otherwise transport our minds
Between necessary locations
Reengineered to become a foundation
Of dance that inspires through motion
Giving us a sense of space
In communities
Of those displaced.

Words otherwise used
To order food at drive throughs
Matured by intellect of youth
From the inside out
Manifest poems
That serve as lampposts
Illuminating alternate passage
Unseen on city streets
Darkened by ignorance
And disregard.

Sound otherwise cascading
Through a cacophony
Of daily routines cuts
Through disparities in access
Like the Sphinx across a history
Of young minds
A mosaic expressing music
Programs of pearls
Depict an ocean of opportunity.

Skill and imagination cooperate
Fueled by investment of those
Viewing basic needs as a right
Beyond the barriers
Built by birth and finance.

Enrichment, exposure, and instruction
Bringing beauty of expression
Revealing the ideas and feelings
Of those whose voice
Fills the opportunity
Permitted by the power of the arts
To unveil our humanity.

String Theory
(Commissioned as Poetjournalist-in-Residence of Shar Music)

A cherished moment
Inside a child's eyes
The confidence invoked
Constructing that first sound
Articulating their soul
Through a string instrument.

An occasion originating a duty
Driving devoted partners
Spirited at Shar in customary ways
Enabling the setting to make achievable
Dreams otherwise improbable
For the eager player
In you and me.

Bows unleashing the potential of personality
Violins singing the harmonies of futures
Bathed in distinction
Violas empowering the sensibility
To connect with one another
Cellos comforting us
With stirring sonority.

Sheet music serving
As the bedrock upon which
Strings are the catalyst
Bringing contents together
Releasing to an audience of one or many
We are more than accessories
To the quality that emanates
From our constituency.

Whether a novice
Stretching horsehair across woven steel
For the initial time
Or subtlety of a seasoned pro
Playing seasons for those
Who feel Spring in Winter
Through the purpose
And passion of our team.

Inspiring joy through string music
Dedicated we stand at the forefront
Advocates in an industry committed
To make the lives we lead
A little better through the artistry
Of our humanity.

The Melody of Parents

(Commissioned as Poetjournalist-in-Residence of Shar Music)

Notes fill the air
Cresting
Against riverbanks
From the fingers of a child
But behind the resonance
Are parents who smiled
Drove to the lessons
That lasted too long
But not long enough.

Getting to the dress store
Preparations
For the first recital
Tuxedo rental
Letting the sounds
Of etudes and scales
Invade the Netflix binge
Rehearsal for the coming journey
Of broken strings
And mended memories
Filled with a pride only matched
By the innocent joy
Of achievement.

A bond built
Through the key changes
And time signature
Of opportunity
Prepared by parents
Devoted
To the music they saw
In their child's eyes.

Replay
(Commissioned as Poetjournalist-in-Residence of Shar Music)

The fundamental flicker of sunlight
Dawning in a child's eyes
The first time they behold
Notes created from what they own
Beneath their chin and bow hold.

It sends an empire of pride
From my heart
To their shoulder
Upon which rides the instrument
Of their desire.

As a parent
I bear the fears
For perils and uncertainty
Which they aren't aware
To be scared of yet.

It's too small for their fingers
A string broke fracturing
The melody of a downstroke
And my confidence to fix it
As easily as I lace their shoes
Before my morning embrace.

And can I really afford
What might be a brief affair
In a dream where I adore my child's
Mind that changes mood as easily
As key changes in a tune in book 2?

And what if that sound is just not right
I don't live a life of soundposts, bridges
And chin rest tensions yet I want to trust
In this array of options.

There is a partner that exists
More than more worry
This screenplay for their life
Requires a partner to aid
Replacing the broken strings
Of my tenacity striving to realize
The capacity of my child's runway
Together staying in harmony
With my budget and their youthful
Flexibility.
An adventure highway
Examining the capability
Only made possible
Through this amazing program
Replay.

Masterpiece

(Commissioned as Poetjournalist-in-Residence of Shar Music)

The lone performer
Skilled and sincere
Pulls across strings
Creating a bridge
As sounds take flight
Dancing and swaying
In the quiet
Of nighttime melodies.

With every movement
Her bow fills the emptiness
Found in the melancholy
Of a modern age
Digitized for loneliness
Only made whole
By each graceful note
A symphony of passion
And mastery.

Time seems to stand
Still sowing a sonority
Of kindred spirit
Filling the concert hall
Of our lives with talent
Echoing in the awe
Embodied in souls stirred
By the magnificence
Only inherent
In this moment
Of a masterpiece.

Music Teachers

(Commissioned as Poetjournalist-in-Residence of Shar Music)

Inspired
Passion and knowledge
Shared through the bar lines
And melodies of magic.

A signature to the key
Of the lives of students
Carried through lessons learned
And candies earned.

The power of music
Discerned through a beauty
By music teachers
More than just educators
Mentors, friends, and creators.

A love for music
Engraved upon
The hearts of students
Like the sheet music
That brings joy and purpose
to help souls thrive.

It is something to state
Appreciate with honor
The impact of music teachers
As a simple truth.

A debt paid
By notes displayed
Through talent and ability
Only attained...

With the dedication
Of my music teacher.

Rosin
(Commissioned as Poetjournalist-in-Residence of Shar Music)

Violin players wield bows
hewn from Pernamubuco wood
bookending the tension
of hair from horses' tails.

Silky equine strands
Would draw no sound
If not for the rosin
Delicately yet repeatedly
Applied disrupting
An otherwise serene interaction.

To create beautiful melodies
Friction between metal and biological
Material must be initiated.

Weightlifters, dancers
Climbers, bull riders
All use sap drizzled from pine trees
Distilled into beautiful tools
That empower ability.

It is compelling
How love for my mother
Only grew like morning glories
After adolescent conflict
And admonishment for my behavior.

It is alluring
How love for my wife only deepens
When a diet of disagreements
Comprise an agitation
Within the exquisite complexion
Of a union destined for ecstatic evolution.

Whether kept
By guard or cloth
Dark or amber
This role of rosin
Seeks to let us all remember
How our path to the harmonies
In existence lie in the friction
Through which we relate the differences
That make us all unique.

Vibration
(Commissioned as Poetjournalist-in-Residence of Shar Music)

Options abound
For the source
Of vibration
Generating my expression
Of musical personality.

As a child
They told me catgut
Brought my melodies
To completion
But sheep or cows
Sacrificed their intestines
For me to tell my childhood stories
Through a wooden appliance.

Today gut
Steel or synthetic cores
Wrapped amidst metal
Tighten to enable
Acquittal of
A fundamental tone.

My bridge carries
Silken identity
To a body ready
From top to bottom
A post of sound
Channeling desire
To communicate in a voice
Constructed from
My vital organs.

An Overture to Thomastik
And D'Addario
Dominant I paint pictures
With Pirastro, Larsen
Corelli.

I rely on vibration
From the strings
Of my violin.

Roadmap
(Commissioned as Poetjournalist-in-Residence of Shar Music)

Hieroglyphs
Human markings
Written chaperone
To the sound of our soul
4,000 years in the making.

A unique order
Intentional frequencies
Calculated to convince us
Of something greater
Than what we can see
Or assimilate.

Otherwise lost
They are etched
In memory
Formerly sand and clay
And now inscriptions
Found on the remnants
From paper mills
On my music stand.

Like the atlas
Parchment from
My childhood
Highlighted with pigment
To illuminate
A path for my family
This is my roadmap
A moment creating
A collective better day
Through my instrument.

Gospel Music
(Commissioned as Poetjournalist-in-Residence of Ovation TV)

The music resonates with a religion
To which I do not belong
But do not need to.

The melodies concoct a connection
To a belief I may not share
But is not a necessity
To be consumed by faith
Of something greater
Than myself.

The harmonies
Move me inward
Finding a piece
Of my greatest joy and pain
In the same moment
And celebrate an acquaintance
With others.

I can't seem to stay seated
The notes dictate that I rise
My body aching to praise
The infectious emotion inside.

I am taken
Within this occasion
To alternate accommodations
In which I cannot reside
But a visit from time to time
Fortifies my soul
A testament giving rise
To a courage cajoled
By the chordal bounty
Bestowed in
This moment with gospel.

Intrigue

(Commissioned as Poetjournalist-in-Residence of Ovation TV)

A deftly torn blue skirt
Dangling from the fire escape
In a dreary windswept alley.

The crimson-stained carpet
Slightly askew on the timbered floorboards
Of a library with locked door.

It draws us in
This intrigue of something
Gruesome in real life
Becoming beautiful in this
Safe space enticing me in a world
Of inscrutability.

Tantalizing
A tragic crime unveiled
Revealing to me an identity
The character I am not
In reality
But in this story
I can be.

I usually solve the puzzle
Prior to the ending
Letting me know in memory
I have uncovered so much more
Than the actuality of a crime
My time well spent on self.

Whether private eye or victim
I am just one of the vaudeville
Cursed cast of characters who frame
This journey that fulfills my thirst
For perplexity.

Ultimately, it is a break
From my day that I all too often
Spend living in quite the wrong way
So the left turn into a conundrum
Of subtlety brings satisfaction
That overwhelms me.

6
ENCORES

Whispered Journey
(Commissioned as Poetjournalist-in-Residence of The Rodham Institute)

Unease
Arisen in the obscurity
That cloaks change
An unknown fear
Greater than
What has hurt in the past.

An opportunity
Whispered through
The foliage of anxiety
Seeks to stoke
Bravery to break
The chains enslaving me
To the safety
Of indifference
And mediocrity.

Spiraling forward
Hoping the handlebars
Of my instincts keep catastrophe
From eclipsing the growth
That give this journey the meaning
That drives the breath I draw
To whisper
The delicious notes of comfort
That I feel are deserved
For my bravery.

The Peace Prize
(Commissioned as Poetjournalist-in-Residence of Ovation TV)

Harsh vertical lines dissect his furrowed brow
a New York Times crossword with no solutions
No word to employ to fill the empty square voids left
by accosted women, broken men and unfathered children
Fighting for the spoils of war.

The flak jacket grips the haphazard pieces
of a man deconstructed from a capricious life
Before war to become a warrior
A reverberation to aggression
Heroes are not programmed
To seek the spoils of war.

The red blanket strewn
Across the broken baby carriage
Mirrors the blood hewn from a democracy
Built from the granite blocks of Khreschatik street
And empty banks and grocery stores with no meat
As unseasoned soldiers displace children playing
And mothers chiding their young
to grow up with honor
As the stray dogs wander
The streets of war.

I bring tranquility to his countenance
Smoothing the chiseled brow of injury
Pulling the rip cord of ageless pain
Releasing a freedom from the bitterness
There is a reason and rhyme for him
To construct the strength for destruction
But I seek the tenacity to stand still
Righteous yet not fulfilled
Honorable yet not honored
By crowds lining the road
Recognizing the return of those
From the battlefields of war.

I crave what rooms with chairs
And strategy can bring
Time always mends the tribal break
History rings with the tales from its heirs
My tribe is the resurrection to another
I see the nation across within
I am the butler to my neighbor's home
I feel the fear of those not me
And roam through rejuvenated avenues
My temple furrowed not with misery but hope
There is a tranquility in soliloquy with another
On the silken prairie of peace.

The ties they told me to make with my enemy
I made with memories of accosted women
Broken men and unfathered children
And the unwise hatred for those different
I crease the paper airplane to carry my hope
As I rise on a new lease for my people
My tribal ease of conscience lies
In history that defies what could comprise
The lives of my children as their children arise.

I am the Peace Prize.

Winter Mind

(Commissioned as Poetjournalist-in-Residence of The Rodham Institute)

An urn on the mantle
Furnishing a memory
Within the cacophony
Of interior design.

A glance in the mirror
Reflecting
The extra toothbrush holder
Empty for another season
With the longing
It could be used once again
But won't.

Presents under the tree
Lacking the wrong gifts
That are only bought
By the right lover
Who knows you so well
But buys just short of your expectations
Until their loss commands realization
Of the depth of how they exceeded
Your demands.

A gaze at snow drifting
Slowly past the candles dripping
With religion and belief
In that which gives the strength
To hold on to a life bereft
Of those who shared
The memories that built it.

A question lingers
On the edge of sanity
And loneliness
"Is there another chapter for me?"

About the Author

Named a 2005 MacArthur Fellow, President Obama's first appointment to the National Council on the Arts and member of President Biden's Arts Policy Committee, Aaron P. Dworkin is former dean and current Professor of Arts Leadership & Entrepreneurship at the University of Michigan's School of Music, Theatre & Dance. Aaron is a best-selling writer and poetjournalist having authored his poetry collection, *They Said I Wasn't Really Black*, along with four other books including his memoir, *Uncommon Rhythm: A Black, White, Jewish, Jehovah's Witness, Irish Catholic Adoptee's Journey to Leadership* and *The Entrepreneurial Artist: Lessons from Highly Successful Creatives*. Aaron originated the terminology "poetjournalism" which he defines as "journalism in which a news story or other event is presented in poetic form incorporating elements of emotion, opinion and creative illustration." He serves as the Poet-in-Residence of The Rodham Institute at George Washington University, Max M. & Marjorie S. Fisher Foundation, Wright Museum of African-American History, Ovation TV Network and Shar Music. Hailed by critics as "powerful," "stirring," "passionate and heroic," and "a tour de force," Aaron has performed his poetry as a prominent spoken-word artist during his national tours including the Wright Museum in Detroit, Galapagos Theater in New York, Harvard University, Chautauqua, University of Michigan, Minneapolis Orchestra Hall, NJPAC and Orchestra Hall in Detroit amongst others and is a member of the Academy of American Poets. He has been featured on The Today Show, NBC Nightly News, CNN, Jet Magazine and named one of *Newsweek's* "15 People Who Make America Great." He has two recording albums and collaborated with a breadth of artists including Yo-Yo Ma, Damien Sneed, Anna Deveare Smith, Damian Woetzel, Lil Buck and others. His Emmy award-winning film *An American Prophecy* was honored by numerous festivals, while his visual digital art project, *Fractured History*, has exhibited to rave reviews.

Aaron is also a leading social entrepreneur having founded the globally-recognized Sphinx Organization, the leading arts organization with the mission of transforming lives through the power of diversity in the arts. He also serves as host of the nationally-broadcast Arts Engines show with a viewership of over 100,000. Aaron is the recipient of honors including the National Governors Association Distinguished Service to State Government Award, BET's History Makers in the Making Award and Detroit Symphony Orchestra's Lifetime Achievement Award and been named Detroit News's Michiganian of the Year and the National Black MBA's Entrepreneur of The Year.

A sought-after global thought leader and a passionate advocate for diversity and inclusion, excellence in arts education, entrepreneurship, and leadership, as well as inclusion in the performing arts, Aaron is a frequent keynote speaker and lecturer at numerous universities and global arts, creativity, and technology conferences and is on the roster of the prestigious APB speakers bureau. He is a member of the Recording Academy (GRAMMYs) and has served on the Board of Directors or Advisory Boards for numerous influential arts organizations including the National Council on the Arts, Michigan Council for Arts and Cultural Affairs, Knight Foundation, National Association of Performing Arts Professionals, Avery Fisher Artist Program, Independent Sector, League of American Orchestras, Ann Arbor Area Community Foundation, Michigan Theater and Chamber Music America. Having raised over $50 million for philanthropic causes, Aaron personifies creative leadership, entrepreneurship, and community service with an unwavering passion for the arts, diversity, and their role in society.

Aaron has a myriad of life interests including innovation, creativity, human pair bonding and is passionate about social impact having founded a homeless organization and a literary magazine. He is an avid kayaker, poker aficionado and boater, having captained multiple crossings of the Gulfstream. He is an explorer of the culinary arts and a consummate movie enthusiast watching over 150 films every year. He is married to Afa Sadykhly Dworkin, a prominent international arts leader who serves as President and Artistic Director of the Sphinx Organization and has two awesome sons, Noah Still and Amani Jaise. They reside in Michigan with their two Savannah cats, Mocha and Pekoe, and English Cream Retriever, Rondo.